"It is the oddest realization that our 21st Century understanding of what right and left signifies, the human brain is wired opposite of that very understanding. Should one contemplate grand design, it might be fodder for much humor regarding our mortality and our much too often implied importance."

~Mike Joyner

Random Musings

of the Left Hemisphere

by

Mike Joyner

ISBN-13: 979-8388978059

Library of Congress Control Number: 2023906151
Publisher: Joyner Outdoor Media, McGraw, New York
Print Services: Kindle Direct Publishing, Seattle, WA

Contact the author: mjoyner@joyneroutdoormedia.com

www.joyneroutdoormedia.com/rmotlh.html

Revision 1.0

Dedicated to:

Those who remember the history of how we were founded and vehemently opposed the tyranny our founders railed against. In doing so, continue staying the course and forever vigilant against those who tirelessly divide us to repeat the history of failed societies romanticized of old world Europe.

Table of Contents

From The Author

Given the title and back cover copy, you may have a preconceived idea of what is written within these pages. If from the conservative or right-wing camps you may have, in anticipation, cheered on in solidarity. If from a liberal or leftist camp, you may have gotten your hackles up before turning the title page. This is expected and a somewhat normalized response. However, without reading a single chapter of substantive thought, collections of random musings, and dwelling upon thinking, neither camp has begun to ponder my intentions or the end-to-end that has taken place in verbalizing these thoughts upon important matters or societal happenings.

Although I tackle some of what gnaws at us at times, complex subjects, some very controversial, I wish to share with you what I truly see and observe in each of you as friend or foe, of the like-minded or intellectual opposite, or ideological adversary. Each of us comes from many generations and varied life experiences. Each of our lives is ours to live in our collective experiences. We argue and disagree on societal issues, how to govern, and what God or not to believe in. We can agree our time here as the planet spins and orbits the sun is a pinprick on the timeline of what we come to understand as Earth's history. Our time is precious and short. In saying all this, I share the same mortality, the love of family and friends, and I want the best for future generations of children.

I offer these musings without malice or hostile intent, only as matters of some reasoned opinion. You may rejoice in agreement or think of me with disdain for uttering them. In keeping with the first amendment, it is my right to voice my view from here as much as yours. Again, there is no snarky inflection offered in saying so. In reading the musings that follow, please take the intended voicing as one from a fellow human who values people, genuinely likes them, life as it is, warts and all, and is fully aware that no single solution to any societal ills fits the vast complexities that exist in our day-to-day interactions.

It is a constant effort, taxing at times, to get along with those we disagree with. The call for civility has all but evaporated in a heightened discourse. What has changed in my lifetime that I can easily observe is how nasty we can be to each other in politics and ideologies.

I hold strong opinions and can debate them as spiritedly as anyone. However, I will not run roughshod over you or beat you into submission simply because we see things from different viewpoints. With only a few exceptions, I have found that given a few minutes engaged in conversation in learning about you, I can find some common ground in our life's passions, vocations, professional endeavors, music, and even foods or well-crafted adult beverages. We share the same planet for a very short commodity we call one's lifetime.

I intend to voice my thoughts on what I view as upside-down thinking, woke-ism, lack of personal fortitude, and efforts to trash what we were founded on in the name of socialism or any other European construct we railed against several centuries ago. Single-handedly solving the current hyper-escalated strife and discourse is a fool's errand, in my view. No matter how much I would enjoy a lasting coming together as Americans, as neighbors united in our common good, I find myself opinioned that it takes a major natural disaster or attack on our soil akin to 9/11 to bring us along past our discourse to act as we live together in the same country.

I'll repeat for the sake of it alone, whether you find my musings resonating in solidarity, cause you relief to read or hear this said out loud, or you rail against them in feverish internet keyboard warrior frenzy, or worse, scream in my face in your "nails on a chalkboard" shrill that you can muster in a display of uncivil foolishness. I can, as you, voice my views in a firm and clear voice and at a sound pressure level lower than the latest generation fighter jet engines. I'll not succeed in being heard or read by bombastic efforts that lack civility. I assume fundamentally that each of you has your reasons and life experiences in formulating your views of the world. We can start any debate or discussion regarding each other as humans.

How Did I Arrive?

For the pure folly of stating background, some precepts to dispel any notion of how you think I may have gotten to this place as a left hemisphere dominant thinker. I'll flatly point out that I do not enjoy a free lifetime membership in the Mensa Society, or for that matter, any membership level. You can rest assured they don't have the slightest notion that I exist.

By today's standards, I grew up an overprivileged white boy. Yes, 100 percent cracker, head to toe. I was raised without a silver spoon, as were the generations in my lineage before me, both sides, in fact: working-class folks, nose to the grindstone, salt of the earth. I am privileged in rational observation and factual definition by growing up in a traditional family with two loving parents who worked hard to have the best they could afford for us with shelter, food, and clothing. I was taught to observe the value in others, what they did and acted upon, not by their misfortunes or lucky breaks. The color of your skin and what boat your ancestors came over on didn't matter. There was great attention paid to your actions and how you treated others. I was also taught that you are the sum of your choices, a product of who you spend your time with, and, most importantly, the crowd you run with. Lame excuses and blaming others for infractions of obligations or moral code were not tolerated. Our word to others mattered, and we owned our actions lock, stock, and barrel.

Despite any conceived notions, I do not hold lofty and convenient opinions. At the same time, I live in obscene wealth, smoking fine Cuban cigars while nursing a rare bourbon that costs more than a cruise to the Bahamas for a family of four. I ask that you note the level of sarcasm as I jest. In short, I was not born of family aristocracies that I can determine as far back as 1500, the year of our Lord. At one point in my life, I came within a week and a half of crossing the threshold of the millionaires' club. With the tech market crash in 2002, a planned sale of an image sensor company, I was one of five founders who tanked with the market crash that shuttered thousands of tech companies. Bouncing back from that without going bankrupt was a low point in my career that I would eventually recover from. I was grateful then and now, and I still reflect on how fortunate I was to land on my feet and avoid going flat broke.

It can be said that I now live a good life, enjoy my passions fully, and enjoy the love of a good woman for twenty-six years and running. In her words, "still on our honeymoon." So far, no plans for it to be anything else. Something to be said for a lifetime warranty. I say this with great contrast as having been divorced, dreams shattered, heartbreak, the lawyers, and a major undertaking in life failed, it has course corrected to surpassing a quarter-century of a deep and wonderful union. In that, I am wealthy beyond measure.

Some of you reading my musings may not appreciate my mantra of picking yourself back up and making something of yourself. If you read my opinions further, open to clarification, it is not uttered in a vacuum, or lacking compassion for how significant depression is, how lowly the emotions are when life knocks you down, throws a curve ball, or you suffer greatly from your own choices. Been there, done that, and never got the t-shirt.

You might be surprised I come from a family of Democrats with some nonaffiliated family. You could say the Kennedy or pre-Kennedy era Democrats. My mom's side were dairy farmers. My father was a career Navy First Class Gunners Mate and a union journeyman machinist after returning to civilian life. My grandfather made a living selling bait fish on the Saint Lawrence River and was notorious as a bootlegger in his day.

Until I turned thirty, I thought I was a Democrat and believed the propaganda, hook, line, and sinker. Not a radical or leftist per se, but I bought into the Republican's only cared about the rich, and Democrats were for the poor and commoner. It was what I was taught, and I never questioned it. In general, I didn't pay much attention to ideologies or politics at all.

Once I began paying attention and became exposed to other opinions, rationally explained positions and understandings of cause and effect, it resonated with my upbringing most fundamentally in self-reliance, moral character, care for others, and value of steadfast principles. Once I crossed that threshold in processing the world around me, my world view and opinions solidified into a conservative perspective.

To state this bluntly, I have little regard for the Republican Party as its shortcomings are no less troubling than the Democrat Party. The Conservative Party and the Libertarian Party, aside from stated core values, are far from effective in a dominant two-party system.

It is fair to say that I loathe the Democrat Party and the unfavorable opinion of leftists, liberal fascists, far left socialist wings of their party. Once I began digging into the voting histories of the Democrat Party, the more I came to learn how offensive their positions were on civil rights and slavery and how masterful they had become in flopping the narrative in a world-class rebranding of a sordid history of their party.

My purpose here of how I arrived is to give a random and brief glimpse of a life of hands-on learning, doing most things the hardest way possible first, and where I have arrived to comes from direct experience, both good and bad, and not parroted from a November barrage of television ads or flyers handed out during election cycles. I would implore each of you to dispense with the constant barrage of hyper-partisanship, the reams of poisonous propaganda and hit the books of yesteryear that still exist in libraries before the continuous effort of burning books and remaking history completes a retooling to suit their purpose.

It would be best to look back at the congressional records; they may not match today's rhetoric. It is not limited to only Democrats, but you will find that what is perpetuated of who championed civil rights and freeing of enslaved people is not who is screaming the loudest, not even close...

Caught Myself Today

A short time ago, I wrote a short piece on being fed up with all the current news and the ever-widening divide in too many aspects of our daily lives, at work, with friends, family, and, lastly, social media. I nearly took the bait this morning. A Facebook friend, whom I am also friends with professionally and in common interests as a triathlete, shared an article that caused me to nearly fire off a powerful counter with an extra splash of "no civility" here tone.

I caught myself... I had a moment of clarity, reminding myself of what I had written and what I truly thought of this person. Intelligent, professional, kind, friendly, goal-oriented, a volunteer at heart, and someone of nearly opposite political persuasion. In short, I like and respect someone, but we would greatly disagree in the theater of political ideas.

The article was highly biased and, in direct language, stated that Trump supporters lacked a brain, not intelligent enough to comprehend multi-syllable or other "big" words—a poorly written piece of so-called journalism. To be fair, faux/fake/opinion journalism is a misinformation scourge in social media. Not so sure that the propaganda machine of the Nazis in the 1930s-40s would hold a candle to what is pumped out by all political parties 70-plus years later.

To clarify my perspective, I am a registered conservative and don't know who I will pull the lever for; it will not be Hillary, just for the crimes committed that she is not being prosecuted for. I'll get back to that... I am more than glad that I paused, not retorted. In rereading the article, responding to such a waste of ink or, more appropriately, a waste of binary data that could have served as more useful reading made little sense.

I do not hate those of opposing views, irritating at times, yes. I sometimes loathe overzealous partisan hacks, not for the opposing view per se but for knowing that it is for power or inciting people, not for a genuine belief. Like many of you, I witness too many mouthpieces that are not because of principle or solid core beliefs but to win at all costs; the party first demonizes and destroys the other side of the other party. The flip-flopping is just a symptom of that. I am angered at the Clintons get-out-jail-free cards regarding the black letter law, an ongoing conflict of interest with the DOJ, and politics first, obeying the laws a distant last place. A DOJ that does not do the job they are sworn to. Had it been you or I, a lowly serf, welcome to Club Fed. When it comes to violating public trust. I am of the hang-em-high school of thought. I don't care where you get your funding from.

I did catch myself and thought about my friendships first, along with that, the order of importance that my concerns are, and what legitimately gets me to anger. It is not trivial.

I awoke again today (not to be taken for granted) with the love of a good woman and two attention-seeking Weimaraners in a home we had built for us. The day started with a full breakfast, and although I dislike working Saturdays, I'll put some time in the office today. I could have worse circumstances; not debatable. Over the years, I have had my butt handed to me and experienced many successes and devastating failures. It is not a perfect life, but it is mine to live. With that bit of balance in my perspective, I'll choose my loves, friendships, and passions over the degrading political divide with too many at each other's collective throats.

I wish you the best of the day and my regards in navigating the mean season of elections.

#fakenews #divisivepolitics

This was a random post before the 2016 election, at the peak of hyperbolic rhetoric; arguably, it hasn't gone away since. -MJ

Heroes

We mourn and grieve over the loss, even those we have not met, shaken hands with, hugged, messaged, or tweeted back and forth. For many of us, those in sports, entertainment, and very public personalities are exalted as heroes. Heroes to us with gifted talents and abilities most of us neither possess nor honed to such a high degree.

Some heroes fail to get much, if any, notice or recognition, or suffer disdain in some maligned perspectives. They are the everyday heroes in uniform who serve us in our protection, in natural disasters, in war, and during medical emergencies. One can assert that sacrifice while helping others is a higher level of noble purpose, and we can agree.

The takeaway is that many heroes are among us; they appear in many vocations and walks of life. Some are heroes to a precious few, some to the masses. For me, my parents were my heroes—my everyday influencers. The heroes who deserve our respect and admiration serve our military, law enforcement, and emergency services. The acts of many icons of public notoriety are undoubtedly worthy of admiration and respect.

On another level, another layer is those of inspirational influences, the gifted; those looked up to for their abilities and performances. Again, they can be worldwide, national, or local in their sphere of influence.

Upon further thought, at a level that we might not realize ourselves, we are influencers to others in our daily lives, even as a hero looked up to by those we might not be aware of. We can and arguably should exploit the best use of our abilities as everyday heroes. The effects of a society that uplifts one another we could sorely use these days.

While it is tragic that our heroes, iconic influencers, talented performers, and gifted athletes pass far too young, unexpectedly, or after living to a very old age giving entirely of themselves, there lies a jewel of opportunity for each of us. As each of our heroes passes, a void is left for applying their gifts, sacrifices, and the good works they set up because of their successes and achievements. It is a noble effort to adopt what you see as the best in your heroes and make them your own. Kindness to others, good deeds, volunteering, and there are many opportunities to honor your heroes through your own acts and goodwill toward others. Heroes give us much by example and much for each of us to aspire to.

Mom Update, It's Late

It's late, and I'm in a place I would much rather not be. Yet as my mother's son, there is no other rightful place to be other than at her side in her last hours of this life. It is my honor to offer whatever feeble comforts I can provide. I admit freely that I am woefully inadequate to desperately solve what her disease has done to her or what it leads up to, the circumstance of her final hours.

I am angry, fearful, and yet also grateful. When my mother was diagnosed with Alzheimer's a little over five years ago, her future looked bleak. The review of her MRI indicated a few months, maybe six, before she would likely lose most, if not all, of her independence. Six months came and went. Her regime of medicine gave us tenfold the time to enjoy gatherings, special occasions, and memories we were never supposed to have. For that, I am grateful in ways I cannot fully express.

I am angry and fearful of a disease such that it does to the best mother in the world, my world. To those blessed to have the best mother in the world, such as I, we know there is no such thing as only one best mother, as there are legions of them. To say I am blessed to have her is to be as understated as possible. Truthfully blessed twice again as having a father of the same endearing qualities.

To think or to have the line of thinking, "What would my father do" is an immense help. I continue to benefit from what he taught by do as I do. He was a great man.

So I am now at her side, a woman I have known my entire life to be strong, independent, loving, unflinchingly loyal, and all we could ever ask for, now stricken to utter frailty and trapped in a shell of a body that no longer serves her well. It is for that I am most angry as the disease betrays her very being.

Thank you for all the prayers and supporting words of encouragement. It means so much to our family in her time of need.

#Alzheimers...

It was very late when I posted this, a few days before she passed. The outpouring of prayers of support from family, friends, and acquaintances sustained us through a most challenging time. -MJ

Grandpa's Rules for Dating

A paternal guide for grandsons.

Permissions to date come from Grandpa and Grandpa only. He is the family patriarch and guardian of all DNA and heritage before modern recorded times. Failure to heed this basic tenet may result in an extended period of judicial "reprogramming."

1. Permission will not be granted without photographs to determine the suitability and general pleasantries and a real-time confirmed background search. Potential female dates must show proof of the family's fishing boat and acreage of land to hunt. Good hunting dogs are a plus. An auto fax report of the family's fleet of 4X4s, including aftermarket upgrades, is also required. This will be vetted, researched, and checked again at any time up to and during the courtship.

2. You must be a perfect gentleman before the date, especially during and after the date. Once a full report is made, Grandpa will determine if a second date is warranted and at his discretion. You represent your parents, but, more importantly, you represent your grandfather, and at all costs, you will be a living example of the perfection of two generations. Like fine bourbon, you will be your best reflection of decades of refinement of our superior bloodline.

3. You will be escorted at all times during your date by senior family members or select officers from local law enforcement. Grandpa may substitute basic training sergeants or other elite military personnel without notice.

4. You will be under electronic surveillance using the latest technologies, including attack drones, with deep infrared imaging (your heat signature will be a dead giveaway for any less than honorable attention to your date), autonomous nano-bots equipped with the latest swarm technologies, and other monitoring provisions employed by the CIA and the Secret Service.

5. Should you somehow slip under the radar, you will be found out, and corporal punishment is on the table should you violate rules #2 and #6. Juvie status does not apply or grant you a single molecule of mercy.

6. "No means No" under all circumstances, and enhanced rules #3 and #5 will apply with extreme prejudice.

7. You will compliment your date, always. You will buy her a flower or flowers for your date with your hard-earned money. Chocolates are optional.

8. You will be dressed for success for a most proper impression.

9. You are to affirm at regular intervals the natural beauty and glowing personality of your date.

10. Her wholesome, virtuous, and godly attributes will attract you. For any other attractions, see rule #5

11. Pay close attention to her mother, more importantly, her grandmother; this is a general long-range preview of who you are courting.

12. You will pay for all activities planned for your date. You may borrow from family on rare occasions for special and Grandpa-approved dates pending the outcome of a family tribunal review. Interest rates may exceed state and federal statutes.

13. Should your date not go as planned, unforeseen circumstances arise, or in general, you will not seek Grandpa's determination for subsequent approvals due to lack of common interests, undesirable personality, or the learning of unvirtuous traits, rules #2, #5, and #6 applies in all circumstances.

14. You will arrive on time (synchronized to the world atomic clock) to be escorted on your date and return no less than ten minutes early before curfew.

15. As a gentleman, you will preserve her virtue and reputation despite what your date may say about it. A gentleman does not tell all nor speak ill of a date that did not go well. Be well-spoken, always.

'Never Let a Tragedy Go to Waste'

With the rabid debate on gun control being ramped up under the precept of "never let a tragedy go to waste" (I still can't wrap my head around how callous, un-empathetic, and politically self-serving that is), it is prudent to point out the progressives, liberals self-serving, wanton desire to rewrite the constitution, to disarm an entire populace is easily debunked by a short review of the history of world nations going back to the days of swords and spears.

Our country's framers and founding documents were based on circumventing murderous oppression by other countries and, more importantly, by those who would wield the power of our government. The framers knew as a young, newly formed country; we could be felled easier from within than from abroad as we would unite against a common outside enemy. The hearts of men and the failings of original sins can be attributed to all the ills of the world throughout history. With that said, progressives are, in reality, not advancing society but just methodically marching back to old-world European versions of government, which the country's founders railed against.

Throughout history, there have been those with maniacal obsessions with control over others, coveting what they own, and murderous in forcing them to agree and side with them. It sounds a great deal like the Democratic platform with just fancier wording. Does a twisted view of the first amendment, free speech that the left will only apply to a liberal perspective and that conservative speech should be restricted fall into what I describe? The wanton desire to rewrite history, destroying monuments, symbols, and documents, to remove all trace evidence of inconvenient truths of another leg in a three-legged stool?

The incomprehensible siding with criminal behavior or lack of empathy toward others of different views (as on grotesque display over the Las Vegas tragedy) is at odds with the enlightened pseudo-intellectual left. Even supporting illegal immigration (otherwise known as criminal invasion of trespass). If they only followed the espoused principles, they would be far better people and could be taken seriously.

Totalitarianism, dictators, genocide, democide, and the very worst of evil in the hearts of some are why the second amendment is essential to ensure the first amendment, our representative democracy, and the Constitution itself. Over 226 years, the second amendment's intent and purpose remain. In that time, society, the value of life, and caring for each other changed with the erosion of a moral society.

The deterioration of morals, core family values, broken homes, divisive politics, and freedom of expression to race bait, create class warfare, to perpetuate civil conflict is a horrible toll we are now forced to pay.

It is reprehensible and incomprehensible that anyone born and raised in our country would ever commit to thwarting those willing to bear arms to protect our families, loved ones, neighbors, and even them and their families, whom we would greatly disagree with. The cliché "From my cold dead hands" would resonate with the founders as the reality of the time and the firm appreciation of breaking free from tyranny and oppression created fresh wounds. We have become far too spoiled and far too comfortable to appreciate what we have, as we should as Americans.

When a party, elected leaders, arbiters of news, communications, and businesses so large they dictate the entire flow of goods and services lay as power-hungry whores in diminishing our constitutional rights, the first amendment will fall when the second amendment is neutered so effectively it can no longer defend your right to speak, assemble, rail against a runaway government, the bureaucracy that has lost its way, or from the ill intentions of corporations far too interested in controlling our every thought or impulse rather than providing goods or a service...

There are many efforts to reconfigure and reshape our country that would be in defiance of our founding and fail in the wisdom of our founders, who understood the nature of humanity, and the repeated ills and tyranny recorded in history.

Any politician or CEO who flails and placates to the ever-changing political winds has no standing in principles, our best interests, or what our country was founded on.

If we allow the erosion of the second amendment to the point of being compromised and ineffective, unable to repel unconstitutional offenses against us in the quest to install a liberal, leftist flavor of fascism, the scourge of central planning by an all-powerful bureaucracy, we are reduced to serfs. Liberal Leftists have been clamoring in the public purview to silence our voices, disparage anyone who disagrees with their calls for socialism, and rescind our 2A constitutional rights by any means possible. By stacking the legislative branch, bureaucrats who do not answer to us, even by force if necessary, as publicly stated in recent times. They no longer camouflage their desire to rig the game in our representative republic as their radical goals are rejected in a fair process by rational and fair people.

Serfdom, enslaved to a king or central government, is what we initially broke away from, the iron grip of Great Britain 243 years ago. Once the second amendment is made less than whole of its original intent as the foundation and protector of all other rights to live unmolested or enslaved by government, there will be no recourse upon the falling of the first amendment and all the other amendments which by design, intended by our founders for us to dictate to government how to govern, how we arrange our affairs, not to be enslaved to it. We believe these to be unalienable rights endowed by our

Creator, not subject to the maniacal whims of elected politicians, parties, or an ideology.

When a party, elected leaders, are done stripping away the second amendment, have no doubt the first amendment, the fourth, fifth, and sixth would be dispensed with post haste. History, in fact, demands it as the natural order of human behaviors is repeated...

Kitchen Table

As I reminisce on my mother's life, the memories, what I miss most...

From as far back as I have memories of my childhood, adulthood...

All matters of great importance to those who barely a thought was a daily exercise of our impromptu confessional at the singularly most important place in our home, the kitchen table.

This unassuming piece of furniture was the center of our universe at our home and likely at many of yours. Where most all meals were eaten, gallons of coffee drank, where the adults smoked (I never took up the habit), and arguably the most coveted place in our home.

Mom was crowned queen of this special place. Master of all ceremonies that took place there. Many fond memories of her and my aunts carrying on for hours in conversation. I would learn much from it without realizing so. For those occasions, the kitchen tables at each of their homes were also deemed suitable temporary accommodations. Our table would be second only to that of Grandma's. In the early hours before work, my father ruled this special place. I am sure it is here that he gathered his thoughts for the day. No matter what good or bad news was to be disclosed, the table was the safest place in our world to do so. Another cup of coffee, and it would all be worked out...

Of all the things I miss the most, both parents now passed, the announcements and the discussion of any important thing that was conducted there. The greetings, the goodbyes, and the hours of priceless conversation over too much coffee are the best.

In honor of Mom and Dad...

Liberal, Leftist, and Democrat Privilege Dissected

Liberal, leftist Democrat privilege:

Liberal privilege, Leftist privilege, Democrat privilege

lib·er·al left·ist dem·o·crat pri·vil·ege

/ˈlib(ə)rəl/ /ˈleftəst/ /ˈdeməˌkræt/ /ˈpriv(ə)lij/

noun: **liberal, leftist democratic privilege**; plural noun: **liberal, leftist democratic privileges**

1. A person of liberal and or left-wing political views.

2. An advocate or supporter of democracy via mob rule.

3. A special right, advantage, or immunity is granted or available only to a particular person or group with liberal left-wing political views.

   synonyms: advantage, benefit; More

adjectives: **liberal, leftist democratic**

1. Engages, embraces, and supports abhorrent, immoral behavior or opinions and violently employs psychotic, anti-social behavior to demean, disparage, and discard traditional, conservative values.

2. Having or relating to left-wing political views. "Leftist radicals"

3. A member of the Democratic Party

verb: **privilege**

1. Grant a privilege or privileges to.

Observations: **liberal, leftist democratic privilege.**

1. Personal, professional tribalism-

   a. Avoidance of others not in 100% agreement of all matters, news of the day

   b. Violently demand political beliefs one holds, and political candidates are 100% compliant.

   c. Can describe or draw caricature-like pictures based on the most extreme and irrational of those who differ from Liberal leftist ideology without penalty. Those not in lock step may not be permitted to do so without law enforcement and civil penalty intervention.

d. Remain oblivious to the richly complex and nuanced views and values of those with different political opinions without ill consequences. Faux enlightenment is often attributed to noted ignorance.

e. If applying for a job, liberal, leftist political views are mandatory in academia and government positions.

f. Activities are arranged to never experience feelings of rejection owing to politics. *See-snowflaking*.

g. Can criticize others' art, publications, music, or research that differs from their own on race, sex, or politics without fear of being accused of assimilating authoritarian, racist, or sexist behavior. Conversely, such criticism is not permitted by conservatives without labeling of authoritarian, racist, homophobic, misogynist, or sexist. Law enforcement judicial system may be resourced.

h. Systematically misinterpret, misrepresent, or ignore research to sustain political views.

i. Commentary or published word on "social justice" one's peers will share moral and ideological assumptions of justice. Conversely, such criticism is prohibited without labeling authoritarian, racist, homophobic, misogynist, or sexist. Law enforcement judicial system may be resourced.

2. Anti-Social Attributes:

   a. Systemic assertion of authority is correct to control what others do, what others have, and what others say and think. *See- Socialism, Marxism, 3rd Reich.*

   b. Assuming inherent rights never to hear any opinion contradicting one's world view. Intimidation and violence are deemcd necessary to protect an ideological bubble.

   c. Feeling offended constitutes a political crisis for all. Law enforcement, judicial system often resourced.

   d. Assert moral Jihad to establish standards that others must adhere to and critique them at will. Having exquisite, enhanced sensitivity to each and every moral microbe in society while using the broadest terms to dismiss one's self-failures.

   e. Consistency, across-the-board moral standards is for others. Deny the existence of absolutes while imposing absolutes for others.

   f. Admired practitioners of privilege at will may condemn fossil fuels and support gun control, are free to fly in private jets and live in mega-mansions protected by armed guards. It is permissible, righteous to verbalize vile characterizations of conservatives. Conversely, any criticism of leftist liberals is evidence of racism, homophobia, misogynist, or sexist assimilation.

   g. Judge only by one's intentions, rhetoric. Unintended, underperforming, or unfortunate results are to be ignored if deemed to be disparaging liberal leftist agendas or precepts.

h. Protecting public and private property statutes may be ignored to allow leftists room to vent feelings. Acts of treason, violating laws protecting classified information, or abusing governmental positions to use agencies and processes to harass opponents do not apply to those of your ideology.

i. Win at all costs is considered moral and just unless opponents adopt a similar mantra. *See- liberal tears.*

3. A member of the Democratic Party

A Covid Group Clarification

It would be good in this discussion to separate the precept "they think it is a joke" from "I don't think we are being told the whole truth, and the government is not deserving of our trust." Both sides of this have their extreme followers to the point of being fascists and totalitarians, and it is not acceptable to us as reasonable people inclined to be civil to each other.

Vax shaming from either side is uncivil at best. Please keep in mind the group's rules that the group's founders support vaccination and other medical solutions to this awful affliction. The best part of this group experience is the empathy, solidarity, and support for each other.

As a personal disclosure, I distrust the overreach, ambiguities, and hypocrisies of the governments (our own in the US and abroad), elected leaders, and bureaucrats. Before I took ill from it and nearly died, I also believed that common courtesy should not have to be told. It is best practice to do so, and if politics had stepped aside early on and refrained from the constant divisive rhetoric, many more would have lived.

As a conservative, I fully know beyond any doubt that the suffering and heartbreaks from Covid are genuine and tragic. Too many bizarre symptoms and varied across so many make me think it is man-made, a weapon of some maligned intentions.

It is my impression, not fact-finding by the courts. The societal suffering from lockdowns comes as a three-pack: subsequent related illnesses, financial bankruptcy, and mental illness leaving more entangled issues to resolve. So often, we go round and round with it deteriorating into name-calling and reliance on stereotypes to grasp the discourse. Solving the problems of the world is not a one-paragraph answer.

That said, this is not really the group's purpose in debating these very heated topics. Like many of you, I read, discuss, and observe a lot and am a continual student of many interests, including Covid, truly, life itself.

Please give some thought to this as we are finding out amongst ourselves as a group that in our solidarity, we share and support far more than we detract from each other. This is our group space to heal, and I have gained so much, privileged to be a part of it.

From the author- At the time, I was a moderator in a Covid Survivor support group and interjected during a very heated discussion between those vaccinated and those who refused, Although I have serious doubts and issues with the politicization of Covid vaccines, I had to get the shots as my near-death experience with Covid necessitated it as a risk assessment, and the founders of the support group were pro-vax.

Have We Forgotten?

Have you Forgotten 9/11? Your families? Your neighbors? Your friends? Your ideological opponents? Is this just an annoyance to your daily routine?

Despite my constant repetition for which I will not apologize: no, I have not forgotten, hell no…

Each day, every day on every news channel, news website, and social media, we get "fuck the pigs," "defund the police," and more colorful vulgar chants or disparaging language. The narrative that the men and women in blue are chasing down and murdering blacks as some perversion of sick folly driven by hundreds of years of racism…

With 800K-plus LEOs in the US and between ten and twenty unarmed blacks killed annually (the number has declined for the past decade), it is not a plague nor an all-out assault due to racism.

We have a narrative that labels all those in blue as murderous, racist, unnecessary, and unneeded to have wholesale support withdrawn for political gains. Have we forgotten that those who serve us see a burning building, a crime in progress, innocents being assaulted, and their first instinct is to go toward the danger, to save as many as possible even though they may never see their loved ones ever again?

Of the 2977 victims killed in the September 11 attacks, 412 were emergency workers in New York City who responded. Out of the 125 who perished at the Pentagon, no first responders were lost:

343 firefighters, a chaplain, and two paramedics of the NYC Fire Department

37 police officers - Port Authority of New York and New Jersey Police Dept

23 police officers of the NYC Police Dept

8 emergency medical technicians and paramedics

1 patrolman from the NY Fire Patrol

Do we fail to honor the lives lost on this fateful day, those lost while serving us every day? We hate each other by party affiliation, by whom we vote for, and align ourselves. We are uncivil without cause. We are better than this. I can remember a time...

Are we so entrenched that we forgo living the American Dream and all it stands for? That we take on the daily challenges for us to live well and in service to each other as it is a tribute to those who sacrificed for us?

For those of you polar opposite to my conservative thoughts that we might not share a strong Irish Stout, I can toast to our betterment in life and the hope we return to the land of united bloody Americans (as the Brits would call us.)

I have not forgotten:

The memories and the feelings from that day have not faded nor diminished. It was to be a perfect bluebird day in September.

The near-perfect September day morphed and shattered for thousands of victims in mere seconds for many, some in agonizing, terror-filled minutes, hours yet for others.

In the ripples of life, our greatest loss is to never know or benefit from what great deeds and accomplishments from all those lost.

That we came together as Americans. We were united as Americans. We still are Americans. Many have forgotten this very fact in recent times.

Those who perished on this fateful day of September 11th, 2001.

Those who gave all to save lives. Heroes that walk among us to this day.

Those who survived only to succumb to it days, months, and years later.

That we are all equal by way of our maker...

This is, in part, a portion of a commentary published each year on the anniversary of 9/11   -MJ

Hey, It's Me

Just a quick ring, just to say hey.

Rolling down the road, any time of day.

No matter the reason, no matter at all.

No particular thought, just make the call.

Bright sunny mornings were always the best.

Cold rainy days were never her favorite days.

Cold rainy days, Dad didn't mind at all.

Those were some of my best calls.

Hey, Mom; hey, Dad, it's me…

More Important Than a Child's Life?

Second Amendment Right Is "More Important" Than a Child's Life?

Sounds absurd, doesn't it? How easy and positively natural it is to cherish a child's life. Mourn those murdered or taken from us by natural or unnatural causes. The phrase "a child's life is more important than your second amendment right" on its face seems whole, caring, sensible, and human.

In a perfect society, in Disney movies, in liberal utopias, it is the most perfect ideal. In the real world, it is brazenly shoved down our throats as the end of all arguments against anyone who supports gun rights, as to argue it is assumed you don't care about children, hate children, and are the vilest person.

As a father, grandfather, and husband, you'll likely not find a gun owner or non-gun owner more dedicated to the lives and protections of a spouse, children, and grandchildren. Someday I'll enjoy the welcoming of great-grandchildren. I may live long enough to see that. I assure you I'll go down to my last breath in the effort and cause of their preservation to live unmolested or subdued by the violence of others.

I would do the same for you and your children, as I'll not allow someone to assault and murder others in my presence without a determined and purposeful response. Our second amendment rights guarantee the use and ownership of the proper tools to end all physical threats to myself and my loved ones, the same goes for you and your loved ones.

Should you come to harm my loved ones or me, I will respond by any means necessary and with extreme prejudice. It is not bravado; it is the feelings we all share when it comes to our love of family, spouses, children, and their well-being. It is my first amendment right to voice that opinion; it is my second amendment right to carry out daily life unmolested and properly equipped in the just defense against those that may do us harm.

You'll not tell me under any circumstances that I do not care for children, as there is no truth in that. If it came to it, I would place myself between your child and the threat as the teachers who were murdered did in Florida, as that brave 15-year-old hero did. With a CCL, my response would have been more determined. Like any other sane, responsible gun owners, I wept as the story unfolded and cried over their stories and their lives lost. The demonization is unwarranted and patently false. It is an affront that firearms were misused and even more so that laws, processes in place, and professionals who dropped the ball.

The second amendment is the fundamental right to free speech, even inciting mobs and seething hatred, resulting in lost lives and businesses destroyed due to mob violence. The second amendment is the right that protects you and your children from repeating the atrocities recorded throughout the history of those segregated, disarmed, and murdered by hundreds of thousands in mass genocides, men, women, and children.

Your child has no rights if a dictator or rogue government decides to run roughshod over us, and we are disarmed and reduced to subjects rather than self-reliant citizens. By comparison, we are a young country and have survived a civil war over slavery. It is nearly impossible to understand or relate to a war over owning others, yet it happened. Would you equate your child's rights to not being "owned" by a plantation owner? Me neither; it is that absurd.

No, your child's right to live does not supersede the second amendment and your misplaced anger toward a firearm that looks scary or the NRA or the president. However, it is that very right to bear arms that enable you to protect your family and for teachers to protect their students, which sadly has been circumvented and neutered by bleeding heart liberals that, in the end, truly care more about your vote, their power base and would gladly disarm you rather than support the noble purpose of caring and protecting your child, your family.

Your child's life, my child's life, is precious without comparison, as our fundamental constitutional and natural rights as humans to convey how precious and to adequately care for and protect. My title is misleading as what is more important in either view is moot. To cherish and protect are both fundamental rights, and neither is mutually exclusive.

#2ndamendment #childslife #2A #liberalismkills #NRA #protect

Gun Violence Is a Lie

Gun Violence Is a Lie: It Does Not Exist...

Anti-Gun Liberals, Progressives, Morally Corrupt Politicians, and Liberal Agenda Driven Press/Media play you, the public, as fools, as having limited reasoning skills and intellect.

Guns and firearms are tools and mechanical implements. Unattended, they remain where last set down or put up and stored. They do not have a soul, consciousness, or free will; they have no more reasoning abilities than a hammer, knife, or screwdriver. As with any tool, all can be or are dangerous. Used properly or improperly, they may harm, maim, or kill at the behest of the person that wields them.

Guns do only the following three things:

1. They function, sending a projectile wherever aimed, wherever pointed, and trigger engaged.

2. They fail to function

3. Over time, without proper care, they rust

Violence comes from evil intentions, impure hearts of troubled, violent souls, from the free will of humans willing and wanting to intimidate, control, harm, maim and kill other humans.

"The threat, the use of violence to control you, harm you or to kill you is the ill intent of man, of woman, and it lives and festers in the hearts of far too many."

A Happy Father's Day

To all the great fathers, grandfathers, and stepfathers that put it out there every day for their families—Happy Father's Day! To those who still have your fathers and grandfathers, you are blessed.

We celebrate Jimmy, our son, who is dedicated to our grandson Ethan. My son-in-law Chris works far too hard and is dedicated to providing for our daughter and grandkids in Texas. I am told my estranged son Patrick is a good father to Zoey. Despite the heartbreak, I hope this to be true. In your silence this past fall, it has been made clear there is little hope. Life is a gift, no matter how imperfect it can be.

On my mom's side, a wonderful man we knew as Grandpa John. He looked a lot like Santa Claus and was the nicest man. I think of him often. My grandfather "Booty," my memories of him are as vivid as they ever were. Endless stories exist to this day of his exploits. In the pic, my grandfather and my father who were very young in these pics.

My uncles are/were all strong, upstanding men and the best of influences. We celebrate our uncles still with us and remember those who have passed as they, too, exemplified fatherhood in the best of ways.

Leroy Harrison, Lee's dad, was a great father-in-law and treated me as family from day one. He also passed too young; he would have enjoyed the great-grandkids as he enjoyed the grandkids. Great father-in-law and treated me as family from day one. He was an absolute pleasure to take him out on the mountain for the opening day of deer season.

Father's Day is year-round in my heart since Dad passed far too young. I wish he were here to see all that has transpired, great-grandchildren, and to enjoy retirement. It is harder as the years pass as I remember so much more of him and identify at the same age while now in my early sixties. My grandfather passed nearly four decades ago, Dad twenty years now, far too young. The loss of my father is deeper, more significant as I wish he was here to see all that has transpired since.

My dad put his efforts where they counted, showed, and did, rather than talked about it. I watched him work two jobs most of my childhood to put good food on the table and clean clothes on our backs. We lived in a decent house in a good neighborhood. The basics were always covered. If someone needed help, something needed fixing, he'd be on it.

It is my wish that your dads are in as many ways as mine was. He would have been a fantastic great papa; it would have been a great joy for him. Things may have been different with my son had he been around to set him straight. So many things would be different if we had more years with him.

I hope that each of you celebrates the observance of fatherhood and spends time with those you love the most. To those still with their fathers, cherish the moments; life is very short.

Voting Debacle in Florida

For those inclined to make ignorant and frankly stupid comments on the voting debacle in Florida, the facts are exceedingly plain and just as simple to interpret for any layperson.

Every vote should be counted, yet it is being propagandized to include illegal voting, non-registered voting, non-US citizen voting, dead people voting, and voting multiple times. For the basis of adult conversation, let's agree on "All legal votes should be counted."

Votes magically turned in past the deadlines, the cover of night with trucks without a documented chain of possession, deemed invalid and suspect is a likely outcome. Not much different than fixed voting depicted over a century ago in the Big Apple, Chicago, and other cities rife with corruption and payola. It's happened so often in Florida that folks know enough to surveil where the counts are done, knowing it will occur in defiance of election law.

As for the propaganda that Republicans are trying to circumvent the democratic process, again, as adults, let's agree there are specific election laws on the books and some newly-instituted in recent years to deal with the exact circumstances of recent prior election fraud in the very same counties.

These counties still employ the same incompetent or bad actors responsible for prior election fiascos. We are well beyond fool me once, fool me twice scenarios. This is willful enabling for a political purpose. The laws on the books can be verified and confirmed as currently valid and active.

For discussion purposes, this is not about voting irregularities or social justice. It is about willful felony violations of election laws and illegal denial of proper inspections for the vote-counting process. Perpetrated by the same bad actors, laws are being ignored, and crimes against valid election processes are being perpetrated. Folks must be prosecuted, jailed, fined, and banned from future participation in these positions.

The rest of Florida conducted their counts in full requirement and compliance with election process laws. It does not require a Ph.D. to understand what egregious criminal activity is taking place there...

Things Are So Much Worse?

In looking at all the numbers, the precise collections and cataloging that actuaries make a living from of rates per 100,000. Can we say definitively that we live in horrific times of crime and poverty? We are not going to hell in a handbasket, we are riding to hell on a jet plane to speed it up ... Do you agree? Do you even know?

My mother was of the opinion there was more crime, more poverty, and that moral decay, the ills of modern society, is the damnation of all of us. Even if you believe that so many aspects of our country have been turned on its head upside-down on an accelerated conclusion to a similar fate as the ancient civilization of Rome, is this true?

If we remain with the precept that one awful or horrific event is one too many, as we like to think of how many gun deaths or firearm accidents we should tolerate, it is seen as virtuous, a moral position. On its face, it is. This especially rings true when the basic tenets of safety are demanded of each other, taught and reinforced. Yet, those among us defy natural selection or escape all law enforcement efforts. To some degree, we apply this across many occurrences we experience. The accidental death of a child, murder, violence in general, the rare disease without a cure, or reduced suffering. We view many aspects of life through a perfect lens, and we succumb to fits of depression when it doesn't rise to that standard...

By simple observation, in a status quo, we should have more of everything, good and bad, by the old school math of increased populations on the planet. More people, more of whatever you select to single out. If we are to answer by the more telling observation of rates per 100,000 or other accepted sample sizes, do we see upward or downward trends?

Given my age, I have a gift or curse, depending on how you view growing up in pre-internet and pre-digital generations. I grew up in the age of newspapers, glorious 19-inch black and white television, and especially fond of AM radio, only to be toppled by FM radio; 33 LPs and 45 single records are an oddity of the past for current generations. This sets up a perspective I would often discuss with my mom. Back in all that melancholy, you got the news at 7 a.m., at lunchtime, and the most important news at 6 p.m. Then along came the nightly news with Walter Cronkite.

If any crime or significant event were at all newsworthy, it would be broadcast on the nightly news. Local news was in the evening or morning paper. We complain about people buried in their smartphones, yet it hasn't evolved beyond how folks read newspapers back in the day. Us old folks are terrible at thumb-typing on these tiny screens.

Before I tie this line of thought together, it is a utopian ideal to have no crime, disease, famine, and full pursuit of happiness. Life is filled with many things, truths, and realities that conflict with our dream-like desires. Like gun safety, we rail against the violent acts perpetrated against one person or child; some might say even more about animals. That is an entire discussion in itself. Now that I have stated this, I'll bring this back to "Are times getting worse."

I'll explain this as I presented it to my mother as she was confident that times were, in fact, worse than they were back in her childhood. It goes something like this: Back in her generation, even up to my own, if someone did an awful thing, got arrested, robbed a bank, cheated on their spouse, and the list goes on, you might hear about it from the Saturday paper, depending how close you lived to where it happened. Word of mouth traveled fast locally and in hearing distance. It often took a day or two to hit the local TV channel. It would have to be significant enough to be put up on the API newswire to get same-day importance.

From those days before the dawn of the digital age, those times have shortened and accelerated with the arrival of cell phones and the internet, and more impacted by smartphones with cameras built in. In a sweeping jump and integration of technology, everyone is a defacto reporter with nano-second access to publish whatever they see, hear, and how they feel about it. Someone can

commit a crime in a town that no one has ever heard of and have it on a worldwide blast in seconds. Couple that with 365/24/7 demand for news content, everything and anything gets magnified to gain ratings and market share. Those who suffer heinous crimes and injustices go to the front line. Our shocked and horrified responses are good business for the news industry. I have an opinion of that, and I suspect you may as well.

Rather than having me tell you what is what, I will task each of you to look up back then vs. now and the rates per capita in those comparisons. If you shape your opinion by what is presented as news in an uninterrupted cycle, I am confident you will side with it getting far worse. Hearing bad reports hourly each day will shape opinions.

As an offhand experiment, 24-hour cycles of reporting what the opposite of that might make us all a bit less cranky, foreboding, and possibly a bit happier about indulging it. It's a lofty ideal as well. In the digital information age in which we are solidly immersed, we can satisfy our perspectives or have them manipulated and fed to us.

In keeping with the rugged individualism that we profess as a virtue in our country, I politely request you do some soul-searching and fact-finding. You may find, as I, that despite some downward trends none of us are happy about, there is a much brighter outlook and view of now vs. generations ago.

Black Lives Matter-Waking of a Sleeping Giant?

Disclaimer: This is an observation of a brewing "Perfect Storm." I'll be satisfied to be wrong on this, as violence, taking another's life, is the end of all our short time on this planet. Everyone's life may not be perfect or even at all that good at times, but these circumstances can and do change, and it is a life worth living. I sincerely hope we never arrive at this possible reality. Enough blood has been spilled in our streets...

You have to wonder what all these BLM and Black Panther badasses and screaming mouthpieces are thinking, claiming they will start their own government, take over states, shoot cops, and murder their families. Assault or kill anyone that gets in their way...

Do these hate-filled folks underestimate who we are as Nation? I understand there are well-intentioned, genuinely good people in these groups that are upset at black/police confrontations, but you need to look at who is doing the speaking for you and how they are representing you. A glamorized life of crime, a sense of entitlement, and victimhood driven home by the race baiters is not doing your community any good or setting any positive direction of real change for a better life.

It's foolhardy to dismiss the sense of right and wrong and willingness to stand up for what's right that is felt by our veterans, deer hunters, turkey hunters, waterfowl hunters, law-abiding gun owners, CCL carrying permit holders... Would it be a fair statement we regard and hold dear the intent of our laws, the rights of folks to live without threats of violence, assault, or murder? Do we not want those that commit these heinous crimes to serve full sentences and reparations? Would it be naïve to think we would tolerate this assault on our neighborhoods and cities while thugs act like animals and threaten all those in proximity?

If these groups that celebrate the turmoil and violence in current vogue are to assess the reality of achieving their goals of harming innocents and murdering cops, it might be prudent to understand what you might be up against once you enact your "Civil War." I'll suggest you are painfully ignorant of what you may face...

For starters, the world's largest standing "Armed Armies" are right here in the US of A when deer season opens across the land each fall. We are not just talking about the largest when the seasons open in all the states; just a handful of states alone exceed the armies of the superpowers. Estimates range from 13.7 million on up; in some states, it is 20 hunters per square mile. My home state of New York estimates around a quarter million each season. Hunters, by their very chosen pastime, are passionate people and care just as much about their families and those around them. Trust me, they will take exception to anyone threatening those in their families and close-knit communities.

How gangsta will you be when you stare down the business end of a 30-06 or a 12-gauge shotgun? Most hunters do not embrace the gangster shooting style and are at least utilitarian in their marksmanship. Hunters are skilled at hunting wild animals in their own element without their quarry being aware. What you might want to take away from that is they'll apply the same skills in efficiently dealing with BLM and Black Panther, domestic terrorists in the commission of felony crimes against our good citizens and law enforcement.

There are some 20 million plus veterans that you might not want to mess with either. They are already trained and have a one-up on you. Sure, not all can dish out an ass whooping due to advanced age or disabilities, but way more in numbers than you want to ever tangle with. I'd be hard-pressed to tangle with a 70-year-old marine (or any other serviceman), as it might not go well. I hear stories...

Do you think for an instant that law-abiding gun owners will stand by while hoodlums assault/murder law enforcement or innocent people? Don't be fooled by us being calm; by adhering to the law and only engaging at such times, our loved ones, innocents, and ourselves are in imminent danger. We are civil, law-abiding citizens who are over 80 million strong. Do not falsely assume we'll allow you to shed innocent blood or that of those who protect and serve us.

Members of BLM and Black Panthers, you may end up having signed up for more than you bargained for. Unlike the threatening and violent individuals (terrorists by definition) in these groups, my fellow hunters and fellow legal gun owners will not threaten folks with violence or deadly harm. It is unlawful for us to do so. It makes us no better than you should we succumb to blind hatred. However, we will protect those we love, innocents among us, and ourselves, and support law enforcement that serves us.

We all want to go about our lives unmolested, home to our families, work, and pursue our dreams. A civil war would be indifferent to this fact. No winners when the dust settles, and the bodies are buried.

You do have the right to peaceful protests, as you should. Nobody is going to tell you otherwise. What is going on is more than that. It is upon good advice to reign in representatives that recklessly claim what you are hoping to make happen, as the sleeping giant of millions of law-abiding citizens will awake to say enough and do what is required of them to end any civil war you claim you are going to bring to our doorstep.

#blm #blacklivesmatter #civilwar.

It has been a few years since I wrote this, and I am glad it did not erupt into a civil war. I don't know if I can say it has gotten measurably better, at least not by the race baiters, partisan pundits, and the 24/7 news anchors. I firmly believe we may get past skin color, the ills of the past, and the vile racism I recall growing up in the '60s and '70s. For me, I would instead stick with the idea of us all having many of the same aspirations, opportunities, dreams, and struggles of the day.

Each Day

Each day as my norm, I'll start the day with a cup of coffee, read your posts (at least those Facebook allows me to see,) make my rounds of happy birthdays and happy anniversaries and exchange "Good morning" with several group moderators who also make the beginning of the day pleasantries and small exchanges of goodwill a most welcome start. It is certainly my pleasure to do so.

I also read your posts, which starkly contrast the reality that life also bestows on each of us in due time. It is a bit of a reality check as, in such a short period, far too many spouses, relatives have passed, friends, people I have hunted with and written about, young adult children of friends, and those I have worked with or served with in my endeavors. They are in my daily prayers. I have far too many friends saying their goodbyes and laying their loved ones to rest in the past few years. Your sorrows and loss are in my thoughts, and I pray that you find solace and a sense of peace in the coming days.

It is a harsh reminder of how fragile our bodies are and how preciously short our time is on the planet. For some of us that believe, getting right with Jesus would be a prudent idea. Because of this, it is unfathomable that we dedicate so much negative energy and time to being uncivil and nasty to each other for the most trivial reasons, especially over differences of opinion and politics. I am not immune from this by any means. I hope I master this before my time is done. Given my medical high drama twice in twelve months, it is foremost in my thoughts. Knocking on death's door will make you ponder many things, including those too uncomfortable and hastily dismissed.

Some are also gone from our lives, some with cause, and some without, some without any explanation, yet are still among the living. It is a heavy heart to know that though they are alive and well, they are gone from our daily lives, and no forgiving will change the facts or circumstances of what will no longer be. This is all too poignant and bittersweet. Having lived long enough, I have had more experience with this than I care for. It is the fleeting wisdom in this life to learn and know the difference, when to let go, and when to cherish and nurture.

Not my Job: I'm no Hero...

It is an observation of humanities, of what is universal in my view (you may agree or not.) In the wake of strong opposition to arming teachers in school, there is a wide swath of half-baked logic, deflection, and cowardice, even to the level of lazy and irresponsible "not my job" rationalizations. My comments are not sugar-coated and may be viewed as harsh. The subject deserves straight-on language, not nuance. This is not an anti-educator rant, as most fantastic teachers love the profession, their students, their work's impact, and their contribution to all of us.

I am fortunate in my impressionable youth to have really good teachers, except for one. I can recall each of them and their efforts on my behalf. It is an essential walk of life in our society and our country. It is a critical call out of an ideology, first and foremost above and beyond the pragmatic resolve of caring for and protecting our children.

I'll put forth the observation in witnessing far too many teachers on social platforms, in the news, that conveying calm steadfast resolve in the adversity of opinions, respect for views different than their own, peaceful discourse, and deliberate, concise response in times of crisis is no longer a requirement, taught, nurtured, and promoted in educator curricula.

Unless you are a devoted pacifist (I will concede that it is a consistent perspective and not intellectually dishonest), the rising banshee rhetoric of educators opposing arming teachers that are willing to train, willing to take on the responsibility of firearm ownership and conceal carry is intellectually dishonest, hands down. It is rolling the dice of natural selection to discard your own personal safety, leaving it up to the will of a criminal aggressor, mass murderer, a predator. To flaunt this flawed perspective in the care of the students you are entrusted with is far worse than being dishonest and morally corrupt.

I'll submit that in your home, should you ever have the misfortune to have an intruder, a burglar, a rapist, or a homicidal felon come at you, you, as any sane person, would want to have a spouse, a lover, a best friend, or a family member come to your defense, putting down the attacker by any means possible. You may not be able to or bring yourself to wield deadly force. It is an awful thing to do and to live with. Minutes of police response matter little when your imminent death is within seconds. In the best case, the awareness of a defensive firearm may cause the perp to cease all bad acts, lay down, or flee. If justified deadly force occurs, the threat is ended. Worse case, a struggle or gunfight may ensue. To cower, to placate the assault is no solution you have any control of. It is our natural right, a basic tenet in our laws, to live peacefully, unmolested among each other in the sanctity of our homes, schools, and churches. In the general public, a peaceful existence may be a hard sell. Unmolested? Absolutely. It is a fair request, desirable and reasonable to be the protector or to have that with your loved ones.

Do you not value the children in our schools, in your care, as precious as you would in your own homes, worthy of your willingness to protect them, or encourage fellow teachers who are properly trained and willing to step up?

My main point is that the same expectation of self-protection, and responsibility of protecting ourselves and our loved ones is no different than what we, as rational people, expect from those entrusted with the care of our children. We expect this from our law enforcement, firefighters, and teachers; frankly, we expect any adult from all walks of life to come to the aid and protection of a child. It is all our job, and we all have it within us to be an everyday hero.

It is not to say you as a teacher must be armed or carry concealed; it is a life-changing responsibility to take on and never to be taken lightly or foolishly. You cannot, nor should not, force that on those who will never be comfortable doing so, or worse, in a crisis, prove unreliable to use a firearm safely or without determined resolve. It is a high-stress situation. To not support other educators willing to accept the training and responsibility is a blatant contempt for the well-being of your students and fellow teachers.

We, as parents that have children, grandchildren, and even great-grandchildren entrusted in your care to teach, educate, promote by example, and have reasonable expectations that you have your students, our children, in their best interest and would employ all reasonable means available to ensure their safety. This is not about bravado, the evil NRA, or the shoot'em'up cowboy of the Wild West. If you cannot support responsible teachers/staff being a first line of defense until law enforcement arrives, you do not have your student's best interests as a priority, rather your ideology, yourself as first and foremost, and I, as many other sane and loving parents will determine you as unfit for a time-honored profession. If you are unwilling to protect or support those that would protect the sanctum of school and the precious lives you are entrusted with, you are willfully negligent in your job.

As one who occasionally teaches turkey hunting safety/seminars, you can rest easy that I'll have a "no harm shall come" perspective while your child is in my class...

#armteachers   #armteachersmow   #NRA   #notmyjob #gunfreezones

Dems floating Door-to-Door?

Democrats have no reservations and speak freely with a fully sympathetic media. Duly elected Democratic representatives (leaders is an inappropriate title, they work for us) expose themselves of their intentions by trashing the second amendment with proposed mandated buy-back policy wish lists, and floating door-to-door confiscation as somehow feasible. This is what megalomania, elitism, and fascism look like. It is upside-down and incompatible with the United States Constitution without perverting or circumventing it. This is pure fascism, no different than stark examples in modern history.

In the most recent debate, one presidential hopeful, Julian Castro, is against door-to-door confiscation as he equates the heinous acts of madmen with "police violence." Consummate politician bullshit...

1-Set up a negative, confrontational situation where nearly half (45%?) of all households legally and responsibly own firearms, by the stroke of a pen, deem them as felons and enemies of the state. That's the ruse they hope to implement.

2-Subject legal and responsible firearm owners to red flag laws with guilty before proven innocent, flawed, minimal due process, mandated buyback/confiscation of legally owned private property paid with after-tax income, sales taxes, and several other added-on taxes. Meanwhile, violent criminals get a pass at revolving door treatment in the courts.

3-Suggest as a reasonable policy that legal and responsible firearm owners be subjected to door-to-door police raids to attempt confiscation. How would they know? In a phrase: gun registration... Maybe now you get why so many reject gun registration in fear of government overreach, and oppression of opposing political viewpoints, the same assault is currently applied to first amendment rights as well.

Out of the other corner of Julian Castro's mouth, he suggests he can't support that just yet as gun violence is also police violence. This is a precursor false narrative, perverted virtue signaling to create a terrible violent confrontation, then wash their hands of it and blame law enforcement for their ill intentions in a quest to disarm a free society and make a grab for more power and control over us.

Our constitution is set up to thwart this very premise, the overreach of a central government. The goals these liberal leftists have and their total disdain for us as free-thinking and independent citizens should cause us great discomfort. Should this full-court press ever see the light of day, the loss of life and violence in the streets will be horrific as this would be the beginnings of a civil war over ideologies, over trashing our fundamental rights as citizens, as 100 million gun owners will not just lie down without a firefight for an unjust and constitutionally illegal action made against them. I pray that this will never happen. We did have a civil war over slavery, and I can't say we should be clamoring for another one for any reason.

Liberal Derangement Syndrome

Liberal Derangement Syndrome Afflicted Teachers, Parents Unfit for either, Unfit for gun ownership.

It seems rather odd that the unhinged and deranged gun control crowd throws in every argument with the kitchen sink and yet fails to grasp that if the teacher is of such noble outstanding character full of purpose and decisive command of the learning environment... would they not be trustworthy and of sound mind and character we would expect, same as we demand of gun owners? 99.5736% are of such character that they act responsibly, and their firearms are stored or used every day without malice to anyone or themselves. I can't say the same for those who drive, play sports, etc.

Does anyone notice that those who are unhinged, without civility, without common decency screaming and blaming everyone else, inanimate objects, death to Trump and the NRA would make for horrible references for upstanding character and unsuitable for passing background checks to become gun owners? They can be categorized as not being trusted with sharp objects or firearms. Liberal derangement syndrome should be a disqualifier for gun ownership under mental health guidelines; I'd support that, as we should be protected from such emotional lunatics.

Does it not bother you that parents are scapegoating others but not for their children's lack of supervision or moral upbringing? Do we not want teachers who show calm reserve in the adversity of opinions, crisis management, and moral or political discourse? Can they handle a firearm and protect their students until law enforcement can be on the scene?

I believe the screaming banshee role model is not good for teaching our children. Emotional drivel instead of steadfast problem-solving and pragmatic skills for dealing with what life may throw at you may instill much better learning adaptations for our children to grow into stable, responsible adults.

As for what is shown in the news, it is not anything close to that.

Riots Okay? A Cracker's Perspective

Riots are okay, you say? A whiter than white crackers perspective—

I hail from a shit ton of white privilege...

Both my parents were white, as their parents, and you might have to go back through many centuries to the common birthplace of all our various heritages to find much other than cracker privilege. No one in my family owns or has ever owned a Bentley, Ferrari, or Lamborghini, and I am not sure if a used Mercedes or BMW is in keeping with open transparency. I come from a long line of a hard-working family, industrious and mostly God-fearing, morally upright, with exceptions noted. My father, up until his later years, worked two jobs whenever he could when his navy ship would be in port.

My "privilege" was that while growing up, I was given daily examples of working hard to have the basics and, occasionally, special treats. Once a month, we went to Burger King to eat special cheeseburgers and get our cardboard crowns. Ice cream was also a special occasion. Most would snicker at that these days.

We were taught the value of people, good food, clean clothes, and safe and sturdy housing. This is not a mockery of those who do not enjoy those things, as we were also brought up to understand that we were fortunate to have a circumstance to meet our basic needs. We were also taught that to have these things, hard work was required; indulgence in bad behavior, drugs, drinking, and breaking the law would result in those things going away. It was up to us to choose what path we took. I grew up with expectations of myself, my behavior, and my choices.

I was loved without question, unconditionally. I do realize some do not grow up with that. Any bad behavior, however, was not unconditionally dismissed, and I knew I had my end to hold up.

I don't buy the privilege bullshit, period. I don't buy into rampant racism, as it is inflamed for nefarious purposes. I go to hire someone; I'm looking at their skill sets, attitude, and dedication to doing a good job. A job well done stands on its own. The good in others is not a skin color. Neither is bad that some covet.

A man died this week over supposedly a twenty-dollar bill. Not a black man, a fellow human, a fellow American. That upsets me as his life mattered, as does each of ours. No more, no less. He is gone for no such reason to justify it ever occurring. I did not hear the officer chanting nigger or black this or that while he put his knee to his neck. I saw the video, and as most of you, it is disturbing; watching a person die for real is not casual and nothing to be cavalier about. His death leaves a void; whatever good he may have imparted in more years of living is no longer possible. Has to be damn hard for his family and those that loved him—ripples in time, as I call it.

After so many businesses were closed and severely restricted for months, now they are battered, burnt to the ground, looted, and without recourse, as insurance does not cover acts of riot or unrest. Only those with national resources or funds stashed away will ever come back. We get this for allowing endless race baiting, narrative-based reporting, and race and narrative-based politics. No one riots when a black officer kills a white woman or any other color. Sorry, but I see only fellow Americans. The masses are organized and incited only when it fits a narrative-based template, and there is an endless supply of useful idiots in the media and Hollywood to jump on board. Our emotions are toyed with and sold to those with less noble intentions.

This is not white privilege... This is us living in fear, living as sheep. We allow this to go on. You think I am so off based because my skin color is white? Try reaching out to the conservative black groups, and you'll find me demure in comparison. Like my upbringing, they have expectations of their families, and especially their children.

Being brought up to value people and their circumstances is.not a color thing; it is a moral thing. It is a belief in people, being hard-working, industrious, good neighbors, and good citizens of our communities. If you support and believe these violent protests and that lootings are justified, I challenge you to convince me that you do not harbor hatred that has been fed to you and that your heart has not been scarred by it. We are much better than this.

My Body. My Choice

That is correct, my friend. (amended)

You do have complete control of your body and always will if the world is as I see it, as I hope you never suffer the ill intentions of lesser men. The problem is that you also want full control over another life you created because you lost control of your body. That new life is not responsible for your decisions by happenstance or a poor decision in the heat of passion.

It needs to be said that being violated and forced upon is a criminal, vile, and immoral act perpetrated against you. The overpowering and complete control over you is not a matter of poor decisions or loss of control. Same as it would be for a medical emergency.

Muddying the waters on choice with imminent emergencies vs. elective choices dilutes the immense consequences. This is not about rape, incest, or those facing a harsh/life-threatening medical condition. Any decent human with faculty of compassionate reasoning can understand the cause for these procedures in these circumstances. "My Body. My Choice" applies even here as some may choose to love and nurture despite awful circumstances. Although inspirational in forgiving a despicable act, I cannot see it any other way but a most difficult and personal decision.

There are multiple ways to control your body and prevent the creation of a new life in all matters aside from criminal acts/medical emergencies. Free and easy conveniences of pleasure without responsibility may have consequences in taking a life. Failure in this should not sentence an innocent life to a horrific end.

That new life... is not your body... it's a new body, a new soul, a new life growing inside you, waiting to be loved and nurtured by you. It is your choice to love and nurture, which cannot be forced upon you, that is your responsibility and your own "choice."

Although I find my view in this to be pro-life, limited abortion, I cannot dismiss the agony, sorrow, and gut-wrenching decisions that so many woman face and wrestle with under duress, and often with intense, harsh emotional bullying from all angles, family and friends alike. This is the difficult outcome of liberated sexuality that was front and center in my generation, and it comes with great life-changing consequences.

A View of Ferguson

The View of Ferguson from here as a Cracker, Whitey, Racist, Bigoted, Conservative Christian

Those are the labels I am subjected to just because of my Caucasian category and skin color. I also somehow bask in the sun of white privilege. In my long wealthy drenched history (sarcasm intended), I hope it rears its ugly head someday, and I can retire in good health. Don't get me wrong, I enjoy good health as I type and make a good living based on my efforts and choices spanning 36 years as an adult. I am not allergic to hard work, and let's just say I've gotten to this point by working hard and making a few right choices. I have overcome bad decisions and fate, which had me at times having doubts about ever getting ahead.

I have never been an Olympic hopeful or busy picking what color for my 2015 Vette with the upgraded engine package.... I can dream just the same. Nevertheless, I enjoy some of the spoils of my efforts and can just as easily lose them should I come into hard times again; we all can. If you do as I have, pick yourself back up, dust off, and go at it again, then you have a shot at it. Color is a poor excuse for not following your dreams and making a go of them. It's hard, and sometimes harder.

As you may guess, I have no use for racism or income equality arguments. Get off your ass and make your own path. I never owned slaves and nobody in my family for over five centuries. I'll judge you by your actions and character; that's it. You want more income, work smarter, work harder, it's the two processes I use nearly every day. I don't owe you a thing other than decency and common respect, as I would anyone. The same deal, talent, character, and actions impress me when I look to hire for my business. Drop the color argument. I have tattoos and have the entire spectrum on my skin. That makes me a little less Caucasian than you might think. Seriously, move on...

I temper my comments, knowing that my standard of living compared to other parts of the world is night and day. I have two distinct advantages in my favor that have none to do with skin color. One—I was born in the good Ol' USA, a huge advantage as far as opportunities go and what we call a minimum standard of living. Not something that should be overlooked. Two—I was born the first son of two loving and hard-working parents. There is no measure I can describe well for what I gained from that. It is my blessing on this earth. Neither of my parents comes from wealthy families or lives off a vast family fortune. That goes as far back as anyone has bothered to look into the Joyner gene pool. This should clear the air of rumors of my blue blood or family ties to royalty.

Like many of you, I watch the news in disbelief, much of it in anger. The attitudes and the criminal actions of looters and dismal race-baiting leaders insult me to my core. Like many of you, I think that the death of a young man or woman is a loss of a lifetime of opportunities and the possibilities for a life well lived. It should not be underestimated what one person's contribution and the ripple effect can have on us all. Based on what has been made public after the Grand Jury, I can assert I would have never been in such a spot, and it is not because of my skin, social class, or some other foolish notion. My assertion requires an explanation, and I shall explain.

For starters, my observation, especially recent live or recorded footage, is that Michael Brown's parents are strikingly different than mine, and I hope that others would say the same for me as a parent. I certainly have sympathies for the grief they must feel for their son. That sentiment stops when I hear burn it down, F&#K this or that, and so on. I do not hear them or the immediate family express disappointment in Michael's criminal acts before his untimely death. Is it that farfetched an idea that being a gangsta in the hood comes with a price tag?

This is where I am easily labeled as an extreme conservative cracker/whitey. Had this been me, my parents, and especially my father (he passed in 1999, RIP), would have expressed deep disappointment in my actions and that a policeman had to put me down to stop it. If anything, he'd probably apologize to the cop for not raising me better. Had it been me, there would be no calls of injustice or burning the place down, looting, burning cars, etc. It would likely end up on the fourth or fifth page of the newspaper, maybe. The first question in my family would be, "Why did you get into such a situation." The message there: Don't go looking for trouble.

In our home, there were expectations of respect and showing pride in our family through our actions. We were not expected to be perfect, but we damn well had better exercise the things we could do within our capabilities and especially show respect for others. They worked hard to put good food in front of us, provide a warm home, and put decent clothes on our backs, and it was expected that no matter where we were, adults would be treated as we would our parents. Get in trouble at school, church, or, God forbid, a police officer, and there would be a corporal event at our house.

There was no free pass at the neighbor's either. They had a sacred pact with our parents, and it was expected to give us a butt-whooping on the spot and then call our parents so they could double up on it when we got home. On the flip side, our neighbors also looked out for our well-being. Decades ago, when I was of similar age as the now deceased, had an officer tell me to move to the sidewalk, the expected response: "Yes, sir." End of story. The narrative and the precepts here that bother me are the uncivil discourse and vulgar display of disrespect for the police and or others. It is ignored as much to say, "That's how it is in the hood." While on my whitey rant, is it not the breakdown of the core family that is the root of all this? Did Michael Brown have a similar upbringing that taught respect for others? Self-respect? Would it be a different outcome? That should weigh on the consciousness of his family.

As a Cracker, should I say to hell with the world, and go off and rob a small store somewhere, then tell a cop to go F#%K himself, and if that's not enough, beat on him while trying to grab his gun, I know from all the years I have lived that I should expect to be stopped in my tracks and most likely, permanently. From where I come from, we call this suicide by cop. I assure you, had I done this, it would not be a whitey thing or injustice for the crackers. On the street, it would be the A&&hole who got what he had coming to him...

Now that I got my bitch on and spewed my rant, I do this on the eve of Thanksgiving, a day set aside to be just that, a day to be thankful. Honestly, we would be best served to be thankful every day for those we have in our lives, as it is all too painfully short. To be sure, not all is perfect, and the daily struggles seem never to end.

As I calm down while getting this all out, I step back to appreciate who I have in my life, how I was raised, to know right from wrong, and to have some understanding of the world I live in. In all sincerity, I hope my perspective wins over that of the looters, criminals, true racists, race-baiters, and the hordes of self-entitled mindsets that plague us currently. I may not have it entirely correct, but I'll go out on a limb and suggest we might get along a lot better if we all had respect for ourselves and others...

From The Fans

Statement from the fans to the NFL, NBA, and MBL:

As fans come from all walks of life, some very rich, and some barely make enough to buy tickets to see you play, buy your licensed merchandise, overpriced popcorn, hotdogs, and sometimes warm beer. Yet, our tax dollars subsidize the grand stadiums you play in.

The majority of us respect our flag and all it stands for. We shed a bit of a tear during the anthem. As we know all too well, far too well, what was sacrificed to allow us to afford the life we have, and the country we live in and call home. Our flag, anthem, and our pledge are about our ideals and what we stand for. There is no call out in any of the symbols of our country or our freedoms against people of any color or ethnic background.

Your disrespect for our flag, anthem, and pledge is misplaced in your protests. You disrespect all who serve us and those who never returned while serving us—our country.

Your false righteous indignation rings hollow as you are not taking a knee for those lives cut short by members of your tribes, your hoods. Your homies slaughter rival young males and innocent children in their quests for turf in their drug peddling and other criminal enterprises. Yet, a year goes by, and you now start claiming solidarity? How many lives were snuffed out when you could not take a knee?

How about quitting your bitching and stand as heroes, as role models for the communities, the hoods you came from. How many of you self-made millionaires head back to your old neighborhoods as a symbol of what can be achieved in this country? Which, by the way, we fans made it possible for you to be so well off.

It took your hatred of an old white guy billionaire "non-liberal" to piss you off? POTUS has that much power over your feelings that a tweet or calling you a "son of a bitch" causes you to disrespect our country. If this is how an elite athlete responds to an old white guy, we're not impressed; you are not all that as the image you project.

It is offensive to us that you do this as very young self-made millionaires off the back of us fans; you got where you are by the hard-earned dollars of your fans who acknowledge your elite athletic talents and dedication to your sport.

You have forgotten that we pay your high ticket prices, grossly overpriced licensed goods as our entertainment, our escape from working far too hard, and the problems we face. We admire you as gifted athletes and hold you to a higher standard for our adoration. We pay to see you play as we pay actors to act, writers to write, and musicians to sing and play their instruments. We do not dictate your personal life except when you manage to end up in jail for some drunken or drugged offense.

When on our dime, we gladly pay you to perform—millions—in fact, to be our heroes for a few hours each game. We attend and watch on the big screens as you play as brief escapes from jobs and other demands that life entails. We do not watch or attend to see more politics. We are far past 'enough already.'

We, the fans, are free to express ourselves respectfully and thoughtfully. We all agree that our sole message to provide to the indulgent, indignant players and owners is: Shut up, Stand, Respect, and Honor. We will encourage this simple message by withdrawing our monetary support of your franchises; turn off our TVs until you remember where you came from and who supported your paths to a better life.

#notmynfl #notmynba #notmymbl

Why I Carry

I carry as there is evil in the world; the world isn't nice.

I carry as I'll not lay as sheep in the company of wolves.

I carry as bad people do; good people do as they must.

I carry as a husband, father, and grandfather; I am their protector by any means necessary.

I carry as I refuse to be defenseless, a victim.

I carry for the safety of others.

I carry to protect those who can't protect themselves.

I carry as life is precious, worthy of being defended.

I carry in the hope and desire to never have to use it.

I carry as an act of personal responsibility for myself and others.

I carry so that in the face of evil-doers, we, and our children, have a fighting chance.

#whyicarry.

This Old Turkey Hunter Remembers

A bit of a melancholy kind of Memorial Day as we remember those fallen while engaged in battle, in service to our country. I am fortunate for those family members who served and eventually came home to continue living with us beyond service to our country. We are grateful this is the case. We honor them on Veterans Day, and although it is today, we also think of them as our living heroes among us. Not to take away from the intent or deep meaning of this day of remembrance as we naturally think of all who serve us.

As a day of reflection, I also reflect on a spring season of finishing a significant contract at work, allowing me to get out and hunt, which in recent years, the timing of my company obligations and cancer scares for myself, my wife, and daughter put a damper on one of my significant downtime pursuits that has been essential in recharging my batteries and keeping me grounded in most things. Priorities being what they may, the turkey and deer woods would be very limited excursions in recent seasons. This spring resumed, cancer scares be gone, and work caught up to resume planned trips and, all in all, one of the best spring turkey seasons I have ever had. Something very special after having so many memorable seasons in a quarter century.

The turkey woods are, by declaration, my outdoor church where I ponder my thoughts and engage in deep consolation with my maker. With the good fortune to do so this spring, I found my bearings and returned home grounded and in appreciation for so many things and for so much that has been done for me.

It is fitting for this old turkey hunter to reflect, honor, and remember these fallen heroes on Memorial Day as it is not forgotten that all that I love and enjoy comes at a price that they have paid in full for our way of living.

Impeachment? Really?

Impeaching is roughly the same as a grand jury indictment, which means nothing without a trial and conviction. Like it or not, you can impeach a ham sandwich by the precedent set.

Given this flimsy precedent, any of the members of both houses could be impeached at first whim. Watch the actual video of his speech. It would be thrown out in trial for lack of evidence.

Notice how the actual speech is being suppressed, not shown. The village idiot could figure it out. The hatred of the orange man is not evidence. Even heated rhetoric is protected free speech, like it or not: pure political theater and another example of wasted taxpayer money to exact political power.

Have you thought about how you might fare if the Democrat Party suddenly found displeasure in what you thought, spoke, wrote, or did in your daily life? It should be alarming, the display of absolutely crushing and destroying anyone who does not agree with them or tow their line.

All one needs to do is review world history to see how poorly the common citizen made out when this absolutism (fascism) was allowed without being railed against, and often the cause of violent revolution. Does McCarthyism ring a bell? We should all be alarmed by single-party rule, rogue politicians with unprecedented powers, and erosion of the Constitution.

Both parties in our history have examples of failed leadership and wrong-headed thinking. Currently, we have a party looking to dam, demonize, and suppress 75 million voters with the insurmountable resources of the government. Would you enjoy the IRS and a host of other government constructs knocking at your door to bring you down in any way possible because you don't tow the party line?

It's called tyranny, and while you may enjoy seeing orange man ousted, your hatred won't be all that helpful should the party in power changes hands or change narratives and decide "YOU" and your kind are out of favor. You may regret allowing this to continue as it is currently in play.

100% un-American, an affront to our sense of fair play, decency, and unity that allowed us as a county to do great things in the past. Suppressing and demonizing half of the county is not in keeping with our founding.

If you review history as to the conduct and voting record of the Democrat Party during and after the Civil War, and especially the dismal record on slavery, you will note the parallels and exact behaviors in current events. New song title, same beat, and same ole dance...

Although this is a reaction to the Jan 6th "manufactured insurrection," it applies to any number of speeches, kangaroo courts, or campaign events. Moreover, with the eventual release of most, if not all, unedited or doctored video, we learn of the extent of media manipulation applied to propagandize a narrative that is now clearly seen as an orchestrated event by the speaker of the house and closely aligned bureaucrats.

An American Crime Family

In my best Rod Serling voice, imagine, if you will, an American family with a career senator dad, later to become president, with a crackhead son who can't keep away from drugs, women of ill repute, and or his laptop secure and surrounded by other family members all taking vast sums of money from questionable sources out of Mainland China...

An entire press corps doing their best at three monkeys; nothing to see here... A laptop with damning photos and emails, enough to rack up a short novel's worth of treason against the United States of America and assorted felonies to add up to multiple lifetimes in years in jail. One might ask where the DOJ is. It's not that any evidence is refuted; it's "What? You can't touch me."

I'll admit I get lost on some of the sometimes-used legal words, but I can read black letter law, and I am somewhat keen on firearm laws, which should be a slam dunk right out of law school to prosecute. ATF Form 4473 is as plain language as it gets, and that alone is enough to send Junior off to club fed for an extended vacation. I tend to use a similar measuring stick to determine if we have several sets of laws in force in this country, in this circumstance, maybe three:

What you and I are held accountable for.

What many crooked politicians get away with.

What the Biden Crime family gets away with without a single day in jail.

Suppose all this had remained in the shadows. None of us would hear more than a few rumors of it. With Senior so emboldened with a sense of self and declining mental state, there is no regard or care for who knows.

On national TV in Ukraine with the Quick-Pro-Quo firing of a prosecutor looking into corruption involving the Biden family. Then we have the laptop from hell. The cherry on the cake is the traceable sums of money going to more than a few of the Biden clan.

There has to be a reasonable law enforcement effort demanded by those of us who refuse to look the other way. There has to come a day when we look past party affiliations and act upon those that abuse their power, break our laws, and sell out our country. We hung people like that or imprisoned them for life up until modern times. We have made the cost of committing heinous crimes against our country lame in comparison, little more than a calculated risk of minor inconvenience.

To Bear Witness

What follows is a precursor to several chapters of "Ten To Life." It reveals thoughts coming from both hemispheres and a contrast of humanity that is not foreign to conservative thinkers. It is profound and life-changing from all angles.

After coming home from 40 days in hospitals, I have been asked by many to do this. As I am able to concentrate more, and collect my thoughts, it will be a lengthy read, but I hope it is of use to any and all who come to read this. To preface, I am of Christian faith, a believer. It matters not whether you are a believer, or believe in another higher power, agnostic, atheist, etc. This is not a preacher's sermon, but a testament to a profound experience. You may interpret this differently than I intend, but there are some basic things we nurture in each other that flourish and grow that are very valuable when we support one another and apply as much positive energy as we can muster, and I hope this is what you take away from this.

Beginning of my COVID nightmare first week in August, I became the recipient of thousands of prayers, many repeated daily for the duration and ongoing. My wife was/is championing it while battling her own COVID exposure and healed quickly with the antibody treatment. I was denied the treatment despite the request as my stats were dropping.

I went from hospital to hospital to hospital and finally sent to Robert Packer Hospital in Sayre, PA, where I spent the next 36 days. I was intubated not long after I arrived. Upon arrival, I was told I had a 10-20% chance of surviving it. I would later learn that the low figure can be as dismal as 3%. Within 30 seconds, people swarmed me from all directions with tables full of stuff I didn't want to look at. I went lights out in fractions of a second, sedated and unaware of the room or anyone in it. That is the only conscious memory I have of being intubated during the entire process.

I am told the prayer vigils never stopped, and I am eternally grateful for all the positive energy and prayers for me to heal. There is no single word or phrase that I can attribute to describe the feeling it imparts on my soul.

I was unaware of COVID delirium, and I got the bonus package and then some. I had no clue it was not real and what can be created by the far reaches of my brain. It is a bizarre and wildly impossible set of tales of twelve lifetimes I experienced during the 18 days while under sedation in an induced coma. My visions deteriorated toward the end of the process and while being brought back, I was hit with hospital pneumonia from being there so long without moving around. It lines up to my last vision which I will share only part of as there are some private bits to this I rightly share only with my wife:

"No soaring above the clouds, majestic mountains, or a vanishing point of light to lead the way. Just staring at a wall full of machines, boring TV, and a couple of therapy Irish Setters that loved being petted. They were comforting a young child getting chemotherapy, and the dogs would wag their tails each time the child giggle at them and snuggled up closer each time.

This was one of the very last visions in my COVID-19 delirium. In reality I was Intubated and slowly being brought out and the tube removed...

As my lungs and heart red lined two times: I spoke to the God I believe in and listed every wrong, sinful thing, unkind act that I could possibly remember and asked to be forgiven. No answer was heard, the room dimmed a little, no response until a flurry of events that happened were shown before me that I could have been kinder, more forgiving, and I asked if I may be forgiven for not seizing these moments... The room began to dim even more, and I knew my last heartbeat was close at hand. I pleaded, "I'd like to leave a message for my wife if I could...*(private)*" I heard no more, I saw nothing more to see. Without a solid mark in time, I woke in a recovery bed to a young nurse feeding me her favorite pumpkin Pie and I have to agree it was every bit as good as she made it out to be."

We figure this all came together on a very hard day when the pneumonia was discovered and impacted my vision. As I recollect this, I believe I was close to my passing.

What occurred next I cannot explain either as to how, or what is the meaning of it that I should learn. A week later, this same young nurse showed up as my physical therapist. As she is very pretty and has very distinct European features. I recognized her immediately from my first meal there. Up until that moment she had never met me before and of course thought it was funny about the pumpkin pie. As to how she was a part of my coming out of sedation I cannot rationally explain. Several days after, bits and pieces are hard to discern as still under sedation verses actually occurred. Needless to say, you can impress me with a pumpkin pie for the rest of my days.

I can tell you this changes you, breaks you down, and there is no lack of humility in enduring this. I have lived most of my life driven, fearless, even invincible at times and left humbled beyond words.

It is my firm belief I was brought back from the edge, given a second chance to do, to complete whatever I am meant to do in this life I am so grateful to have.

I cannot thank enough my care givers in how they treated me with dignity, even though I was reduced to the bodily functions of a toddler. I will long remember the kindness, the prayers, and the critical support during my darkest hours, and I can promise without reservation I'll make good on it.

Post Fauci Genocide

Now that we have arrived at the other side, post crisis of the pandemic, with all that has been revealed in harsh contrast, hypocritical and smacking of official, government-sanctioned deception and outright untruths, how are we to feel about it, what do we do about it? Hundreds of thousands have died as a result of the weaponized virus itself.

We were told all these restrictions would prevent transmission. The vaccines would stop us from getting it. How much backpedaling and political speak do we get now, tolerate the purposeful untruths, and no one goes to jail for the harm they inflict? Businesses shuttered from the lockdowns, the fallout from isolation, mental illness, and acute depression across all age classes. Do we not have an opinion from the out in out fascism applied by the elected people who were supposed to govern as our servants? We quickly learned how we are seen as servants to be ruled and controlled. Now we know we were fed a bowl of excrement to gain compliance. That our own country back-doored funded gain-of-function research despite laws/moratoriums against it, the infamous Dr. Fauci is still walking among us as a free man. Although a point figure, you can be assured that this sordid deception was orchestrated by more than one person, all the way to ivory towers and in play over several administrations.

How angry should we be over this? I had friends succumb to it, know of other acquaintances casually that I will never get to know better, and know many more suffering long-term difficulties having survived it. I have my recovery that may take several years to recuperate fully. Am I grateful? Humbled? Yes, and yes, to the level of all that I can muster. Lucky to be alive has a most profound meaning looking in the rearview mirror.

What I am not grateful for, or feel any homage to, is the evidence pointing to a virus that was manmade, weaponized through illegal and banned research (In the USA), despite moratoriums in place. That we had a hand in directly funding it through back channels that would make any money laundering operation proud. I have no warm glowing emotions for the half-truths or untruths permeated to justify the lockdowns, isolation, and inflicted societal harm and economic harm to small businesses, especially.

Although I can't dismiss any of this, I also have to acknowledge we should have always followed some precautions during every outbreak, flu season, etc. My contempt for what is being learned now and suspected of early on won't bring back those lost or be of any comfort to those still suffering the aftermath. Due to my risk assessment, I had to take the vaccine shots, sick each time, and now we learn more and more about deaths, heart damage, and severe side effects. I can't take the shots back... Although the vaccine shots may save me from a near-death champion match fight with the virus, they may also cause my end. It is of little comfort.

What galls my thoughts when I think of this is how many people would have gotten the vaccine had it been presented straight up, no BS, this is this, this is that. It won't keep you from getting it, but it most likely saves you from dying in all known scenarios. Same with cloth masks that don't do anything in comparison to surgical or N95 variants. As someone who is not an anti-vaxer, I would not have questioned it as I did, and there was plenty of evidence to suggest something was very troubling about it and how they rolled it out. We may never know the truth, and people died because of it.

A Daily Opinion

As I move on from a subject of concern or controversy that catches my attention, I eventually swing back to what order of importance matters in my daily tasks, my loved ones, extended family, and friends. As I settle each of them in order of importance, I find most topics sink to the bottom when it concerns what is most important. That is universally true until it affects those near and dear to each of us. So, what doctorate thesis do we assign to dance on that thin line?

Suppose I refer to the founding of our country, a collection of bold and self-reliant men and women who made it work, somewhere along the line, the megalomania of power over others came along as evident in other societies, other constructs of self-governing. In doing so, I am often frustrated with what can pass unanswered, unchallenged, and unquestioned. Usually, if I feel collected in my thoughts, I post these musings on social media or as a blog post. I mentioned early on in this book that I voice these opinions without any snarky retort, without ill intentions toward anyone.

I fully expect for some; it may press a button or two. In general terms, I do not set out in my day full of tasks to accomplish, to trigger anyone, or appeal to the absurd self-indulgence of woke-isms. I take exception to the assertion that you have first amendment rights to speak your voice, then seek to deny mine in the following sentence. Using the bureaucracy, the government, and the legal system to silence anyone who debates your positions.

Without further explanation, I would still view each of you as human, a fellow American Citizen, those I share a short time on the planet with. I refrain from seeing others as minions for their party as I have grown to a disapproving and critical opinion of most political parties, and I would submit they do not serve us well on either side of the aisle.

With a new lease on life, I seek to find what my creator has meant for me to do. I hope I recognize it long before it must bite me in the rear end or slap me upside my dense skull. Thank you for your time in following along, and I bid each of you generously in good health and a life well lived...

Credits & Contributions

Lee Joyner & Carol Thompson- Pointing out my mistreatments of the keyboard, dyslexic typing, and butchering of the English language. Reviewing my stories and keeping me from telling too many falsehoods.

About the Author

In his most meaningful endeavors, he is a husband, father, and grandfather to six grandchildren thus far. Professionally, he is an author, entrepreneur, image sensor design/layout engineer, PCB designer, self-professed weekend warrior, turkey hunter, outdoorsman, musician, and photographer.

The author owns a technology company and appears on dozens of US and worldwide video/image sensor innovations patents. He spends quality time in his turkey woods sanctuary known as the "J" Ranch in McGraw, New York, where he lives with his wife, Lee.

Visit his personal website: www.mikejoyner.com

Additional Titles
By Mike Joyner

Hills of Truxton

Tales from the Turkey Woods

Grand Days in the Turkey Woods

Ten To Life

A Walk in the Turkey Woods

Upcoming Releases

D.D. Adams

Empire Limb Hangers

Tales from the Roost

Reapercide

Old Turkey Tree

Roost trees & Strutting Grounds

Brought to you by:

ISBN 979-8-3889-7805-9
90000>
9 798388 978059

www.ingramcontent.com/pod-product-compliance
Lightning Source LLC
Chambersburg PA
CBHW070900250726
48662CB00003B/1484